Reading STREET

Program Authors

Peter Afflerbach

Camille Blachowicz

Candy Dawson Boyd

Elena Izquierdo

Connie Juel

Edward Kame'enui

Donald Leu

Jeanne R. Paratore

P. David Pearson

Sam Sebesta

Deborah Simmons

Alfred Tatum

Sharon Vaughn

Susan Watts Taffe

Karen Kring Wixson

PEARSON

Glenview, Illinois • Boston, Massachusetts • Chandler, Arizona •
Upper Saddle River, New Jersey

We dedicate Reading Street to
Peter Jovanovich.

His wisdom, courage,
and passion for education
are an inspiration to us all.

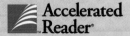

About the Cover Artist
Rob Hefferan likes to reminisce about the simple life he had as a child growing up in Cheshire, when his biggest worry was whether to have fish fingers or Alphabetti Spaghetti for tea. The faces, colors, and shapes from that time are a present-day inspiration for his artwork.

ISBN-13: 978-0-328-48105-7
ISBN-10:   0-328-48105-X
6 7 8 9 10 V011 14 13 12 11

CC1

Dear Reader,

Wow! School has started! Did you know that we are about to take a trip along Reading Street? AlphaBuddy and your very own book, *My Skills Buddy,* will be with you for the whole trip.

Let's get ready. Pack your thinking caps. On Reading Street we will be busy learning to read and write and think. It will be hard work, but it will be fun.

You will meet lots of interesting characters. We'll make a stop in Trucktown too.

As AlphaBuddy likes to say, "Let's get this show on the road!"

Sincerely,
The Authors

Unit 1 Contents

All Together Now

? How do we live, work, and play together?

Week 1

Big Book

Animal Fantasy • Social Studies
The Little School Bus by Carol Roth

Week 2

Unit 1 Contents

Week 5

Big Book

Week 6

Big Book

**Don Leu
The Internet Guy**

Right before our eyes, the nature of reading and learning is changing. The Internet and other technologies create new opportunities, new solutions, and new literacies. New reading comprehension skills are required online. They are increasingly important to our students and our society.

Those of us on the Reading Street team are here to help you on this new, and very exciting, journey.

See It!

- Big Question Video

- Concept Talk Video

- Envision It! Animations

- eReaders

Hear It!

- *Sing with Me Animations*

- eSelections

Adam and Kim **play at the beach.**

- Grammar Jammer

Concept Talk Video

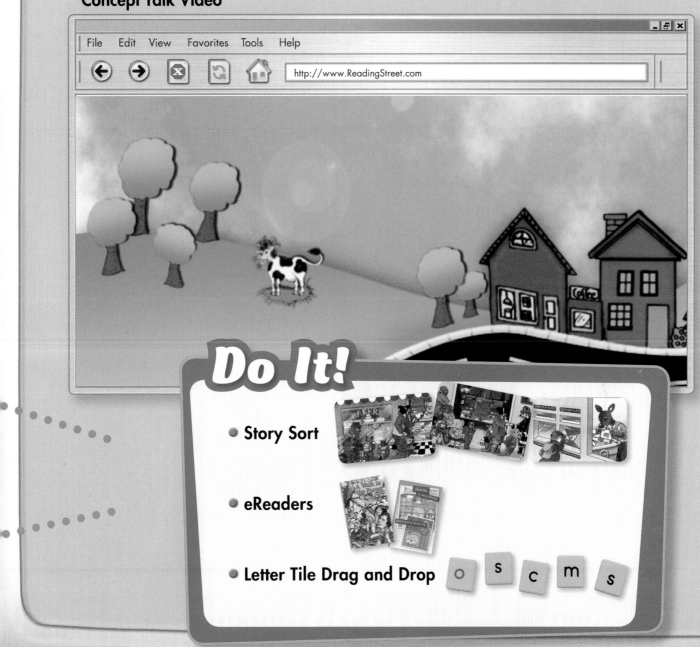

Do It!

- Story Sort
- eReaders
- Letter Tile Drag and Drop   o s c m s

All Together Now

How do we live, work, and play together?

Objectives
● Say rhymes for words that are said to you. ● Tell the difference between a pair of words that rhyme and a pair of words that do not rhyme.

Let's Listen for

Rhyming Words

Read Together

● Find things that rhyme.

■ What rhymes with *man*? with *mop*? with *coat*? with *book*?

▲ Which word pairs rhyme: *nap/lap, cook/coat, boat/goat*?

READING STREET ONLINE
BIG QUESTION VIDEO
www.ReadingStreet.com

12

Objectives

● Point out parts of a story including where it takes place, the characters, and the main events. ● Describe characters in a story and why they act the way they do.

Comprehension

Envision It!

Literary Elements

READING STREET ONLINE
ENVISION IT! ANIMATIONS
www.ReadingStreet.com

Characters

Setting

14

Plot

15

Envision It! | Letters to Know

Aa

Read Together

astronaut

Bb

baby

READING STREET ONLINE
ALPHABET CARDS
www.ReadingStreet.com

Letter Recognition

Letters I Know

Words I Can Read

I

am

Sentences I Can Read

1. I am .

2. I am ☺ .

17

 **Objectives**
● Know upper- and lower-case letters. ● Know and read at least 25 often-used words.

Phonics

I Can Read!

Decodable Reader

● Letter Recognition
  Aa
  Bb
  Cc
  Dd
  Ee

■ High-Frequency Words
  I
  am

▲ Read the story.

READING STREET ONLINE
DECODABLE eREADERS
www.ReadingStreet.com

Who Am I?

Written by Bob Atkins
Illustrated by Yvette Pierre

Decodable Reader 1

 I am Ann.

I am Ben.

I am Cam.

I am Dot.

I am Ed.

I am Emma.

I am Dad.

Objectives
● Point out parts of a story including where it takes place, the characters, and the main events. ● Tell in your own words a main event from a story read aloud. ● Retell or act out important events of a story.

Envision It! | Retell

Carol Roth
The Little School Bus
Illustrated by
Pamela Paparone

Big Book

 1

2

3

4

5

6

Think, Talk, and Write

1. How do you get to school? Text to Self

2. Which is a character from *The Little School Bus*?  Character

3. Look back and write.

Let's Learn It!

Vocabulary
● Talk about the pictures.
■ Which do you use?

Listening and Speaking
● Point to the picture of the bus.
■ Cover the picture of the bus with your hand.
▲ Pretend to drive a bus.

Vocabulary

Words for Transportation

bus

car

van

bike

Follow Directions

Be a good listener!

Objectives
- Ask and answer questions about texts read aloud.
- Point out parts of a story including where it takes place, the characters, and the main events.
- Tell in your own words a main event from a story read aloud.

Let's Practice It!

Myth

- Listen to the myth.
- How does it begin?
- Who is King Midas?
- How does King Midas get the "golden touch"?
- What lesson does King Midas learn?

King Midas and the Golden Touch

1

2

Objectives
● Point out the syllables, or parts, in words you say.

Let's Listen for

Syllables

● Point to a picture, say the word, and clap for each part, or syllable, you hear.

■ Which words have one part, or syllable?

▲ Which words have more than one part, or syllable?

Read Together

32

33

Objectives
• Point out parts of a story including where it takes place, the characters, and the main events.

Comprehension

Envision It!

Literary Elements

**READING STREET ONLINE
ENVISION IT! ANIMATIONS**
www.ReadingStreet.com

Characters

Setting

34

Plot

Envision It! | Letters to Know

Cc
cactus

Dd
dolphin

Ee
escalator

Ff
fountain

Gg
goose

Hh
helicopter

Ii
igloo

Read Together

Print Awareness

Letter Recognition

Letters I Know

Cc Dd Ee

Ff Gg Hh

Ii

cab

The cab is yellow.

Words I Can Read

I

am

Sentences I Can Read

1. I am .

2. Am I ?

Objectives
● Know upper- and lower-case letters. ● Know and read at least 25 often-used words.

Phonics

I Can Read!

Decodable Reader

● Letter Recognition
Ff
Gg
Hh
Ii
Jj
Kk
Ll

■ High-Frequency Words
I
am

▲ Read the story.

Decodable Reader
2

Am I?

Written by George Helm
Illustrated by Tori Wheaton

I am Jan.

Am I Fran?

I am Len.

Am I Ken?

I am Kim.

Am I Hanna?

I am Gus.

Objectives

- Tell in your own words a main event from a story read aloud. • Retell or act out important events of a story.
- Connect what you read to your own experiences, to other things you have read or heard, and to the world around you.

Envision It! | Retell

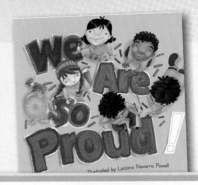

Big Book

READING STREET ONLINE
STORY SORT
www.ReadingStreet.com

Think, Talk, and Write

1. How do we work and play together? **Text to Self**

2. Where does the story *We Are So Proud!* take place?

 Setting

3. Look back and write.

Let's Learn It!

Vocabulary

● What do you see that is red?

■ What do you see that is white?

▲ What do you see that is blue?

Listening and Speaking

● Where does the story take place?

■ What is your favorite part of the story? Why?

▲ Who is your favorite character in the story? Why?

48

Vocabulary

Color Words

red

white

blue

Respond to Literature
Drama

Carol Roth
The Little
School Bus
Illustrated by
Pamela Paparone

Be a good
speaker!

The United States Flag

Let's Practice It!

Expository Text

● Listen to the selection.

■ What is this selection about?

▲ How are the two flags alike? How are they different?

★ Why does the U.S. flag have 13 stripes?

♥ What do the 50 stars on the U.S. flag stand for?

U.S. Flag Today

50

First U.S. Flag

Objectives
- Point out groups of spoken words that begin with the same sound.
- Say the sound at the beginning of spoken one-syllable words.

Phonemic Awareness

Let's Listen for

Initial Sounds

● Point to something that begins like *pig*. Say the word. Say the beginning sound.

■ Find other things in the picture that begin like *pig*. Say the words.

▲ Say these words: *pie, pumpkin, pepper*. Do they begin the same? What about *pears, cakes, apples*?

Read Together

READING STREET ONLINE
BIG QUESTION VIDEO
www.ReadingStreet.com

52

Envision It!

Sequence

READING STREET ONLINE
ENVISION IT! ANIMATIONS
www.ReadingStreet.com

54

55

Letter Recognition

Letters I Know

Jj Kk Ll

Mm Nn

Oo Pp

Envision It! | Letters to Know

Read Together

Jj
jaguar

Kk
koala

Ll
lemon

Mm
motorcycle

Nn
nest

Oo
otter

Pp
penguin

READING STREET ONLINE
ALPHABET CARDS
www.ReadingStreet.com

mop

The mop is wet.

56

Words I Can Read

the

little

Sentences I Can Read

1. I am little.

2. I am the little .

Objectives
• Know upper- and lower-case letters. • Know and read at least 25 often-used words.

Phonics

I Can Read!

Decodable Reader

● Letter Recognition
Mm
Nn
Oo
Pp
Qq
Rr
Ss

■ High-Frequency Words
I
am
the
little

▲ Read the story.

Decodable Reader 3

The Little Toys

Written by Roger Jons
Illustrated by Scott Salinski

I am the little robot.

 I am the little puzzle.

I am the little queen.

I am the little octopus.

I am the little train.

I am the little block.

I am the little spaceship.

Objectives
● Tell in your own words a main event from a story read aloud. ● Describe the events of a story in order.

Envision It! Retell

Big Book

1

2

3

4

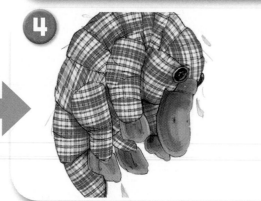

5

Plaidypus
please return to
Grandmas house
112
Oak St.

6

READING STREET ONLINE
STORY SORT
www.ReadingStreet.com

66

Think, Talk, and Write

1. How do you help your family? Text to Self

2. What happens first in the story? What happens last?

Sequence

3. Look back and write.

Objectives
● Listen closely to speakers by facing them and asking questions to help you better understand the information. ● Identify and put pictures of objects into groups.

Let's Learn It!

Vocabulary

● Look around for squares and circles.

■ Look around for triangles and rectangles.

▲ Which shape is your favorite?

Listening and Speaking

● Name the words that rhyme.

Vocabulary

Words for Shapes

square

circle

triangle

rectangle

68

Listen for Rhyme and Rhythm

Be a good listener!

69

Let's Practice It!

Fable

● Listen to the fable.

■ Why does the shepherd boy cry "Wolf!" the first two times?

▲ What lesson does the shepherd boy learn? Has anything like this ever happened to you? Tell about it.

★ What do you think the shepherd boy might do next?

♥ A moral is a lesson learned. What new expression does this fable teach you?

The Boy Who Cried Wolf!

70

Objectives
- Point out groups of spoken words that begin with the same sound.
- Say the sound at the beginning of spoken one-syllable words.

Let's Listen for

Initial Sounds

Read Together

- ● Point to the pig in the puddle. Say "a pig in a puddle." What sound do you hear repeated?

- ■ Point to the man with the mouse. Say "a man with a mouse." What sound is repeated?

- ▲ Find things that begin with /b/, /d/, /k/, /p/, and /m/.

- ★ Name two things that begin like *ball*, *desk*, *key*, *pen*, and *met*.

72

Envision It!

Classify and Categorize

READING STREET ONLINE
ENVISION IT! ANIMATIONS
www.ReadingStreet.com

74

Envision It! Letters to Know

Read Together

Qq
queen

Rr
river

Ss
salamander

Tt
turtle

Uu
umbrella

Vv
volcano

Print Awareness

Letter Recognition

Letters I Know

Q q   R r   S s

T t   U u   V v

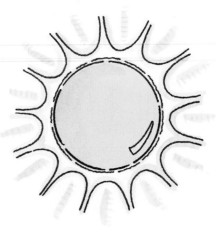

sun

The sun is hot.

High-Frequency Words

Words I Can Read

the

little

Sentences I Can Read

1. Am I little?

2. I am the little .

Phonics

I Can Read!

Decodable Reader

● Letter Recognition
Tt
Uu
Vv
Ww
Xx
Yy
Zz

■ High-Frequency Words
I
am
the
little

▲ Read the story.

At the Zoo

Written by Nitty Jones
Illustrated by Amy Sparks

Decodable Reader 4

I am the little walrus.

 I am the little tiger.

I am the little yak.

I am the little ox.

I am the little rhino.

I am the little zebra.

I am the little umbrella bird.

Objectives
● Identify and put pictures of objects into groups. ● Tell in your own words a main event from a story read aloud. ● Retell or act out important events of a story.

Envision It! Retell

Big Book

READING STREET ONLINE
STORY SORT
www.ReadingStreet.com

Think, Talk, and Write

1. Who helps in our town?

Text to World

2. Which things belong together?

Classify and Categorize

3. Look back and write.

Objectives
● Understand and use new words that name positions. ● Share information and ideas by speaking clearly and using proper language. ● Follow rules for discussions, including taking turns and speaking one at a time.

Let's Learn It!

Vocabulary

● Talk about the pictures.

■ Where do you go in your neighborhood?

Listening and Speaking

▲ What is your favorite color? Why do you like it?

Vocabulary

Location Words

library

park

school

post office

Tell About Me

Be a good speaker!

Curry Veggie Dip

Step 1

Let's Practice It!

Recipe

● Listen to the recipe.

■ What is the third step in the recipe?

▲ Which words in the recipe name actions for you to do?

★ Why do people read recipes?

Curry Powder

Step 2

Step 3

Step 4

91

Objectives
- Point out groups of spoken words that begin with the same sound.
- Say the sound at the beginning of spoken one-syllable words.

Let's Listen for

Initial Sounds

Read Together

● Point to the man in the ticket booth. Say "Man makes money." What sound do you hear at the beginning of those words?

▲ Find three things in the picture that begin with /m/.

★ Name other words that begin with /m/.

READING STREET ONLINE
BIG QUESTION VIDEO
www.ReadingStreet.com

92

Objectives
● Point out parts of a story including where it takes place, the characters, and the main events. ● Describe characters in a story and why they act the way they do.

Comprehension

Envision It!

Literary Elements

**READING STREET ONLINE
ENVISION IT! ANIMATION**
www.ReadingStreet.com

Characters

Setting

94

Plot

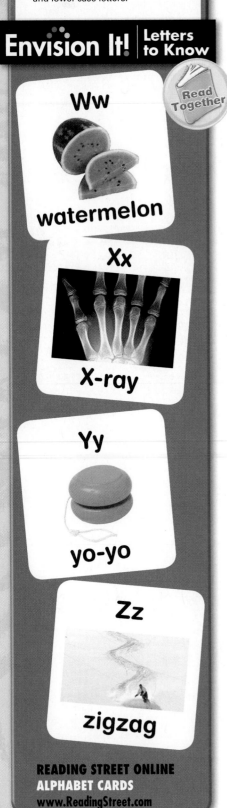

Envision It! | Letters to Know

Read Together

Ww
watermelon

Xx
X-ray

Yy
yo-yo

Zz
zigzag

READING STREET ONLINE
ALPHABET CARDS
www.ReadingStreet.com

Print Awareness

Letter Recognition

Letters I Know

W w X x

Y y Z z

fox

The fox is red.

Words I Can Read

to

a

Sentences I Can Read

1. I am a  .

2. I  to a .

97

Objectives
● Know upper- and lower-case letters. ● Point out the common sounds that letters stand for. ● Know and read at least 25 often-used words.

Phonics

I Can Read!

Decodable Reader

● Consonant Mm (with rebus)
monkey
mule
mouse
minnow
moth
mole
moose

■ High-Frequency Words
I
am
a
little

▲ Read the story.

READING STREET ONLINE
DECODABLE eREADERS
www.ReadingStreet.com

Decodable Reader 5

Animal Friends

Written by Phil Morton
Illustrated by Julie Word

I am a little monkey.

I am a little mule.

 I am a little mouse.

I am a little minnow.

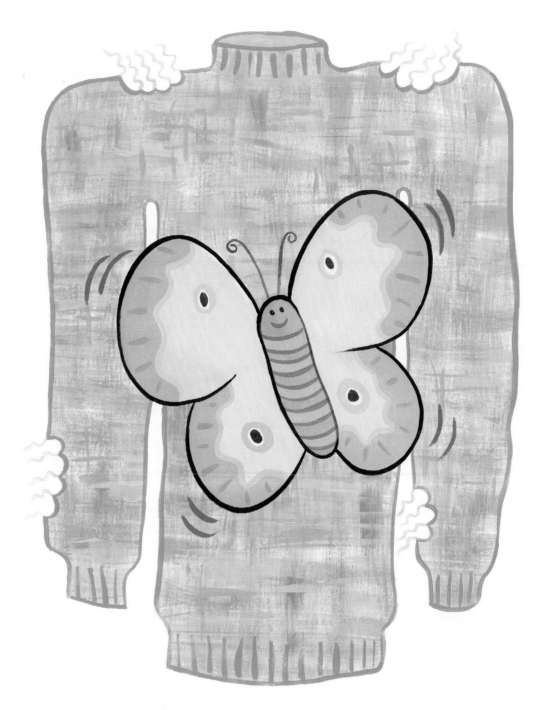

I am a little moth.

I am a little mole.

I am a little moose.
Am I little?

Objectives

- Point out parts of a story including where it takes place, the characters, and the main events. • Tell in your own words a main event from a story read aloud. • Describe characters in a story and why they act the way they do.

Envision It! | Retell

Big Book

**READING STREET ONLINE
STORY SORT**
www.ReadingStreet.com

106

Think, Talk, and Write

1. What do you do with your friends? **Text to Self**

2. Which is a character from *Smash! Crash!*? ⊙ **Character**

3. Look back and write.

Vocabulary

● Talk about the pictures.

■ Put your hand up . . . now down.

▲ Put your hand in your pocket. Now take it out.

Listening and Speaking

● Make an announcement.

■ Listen to a classmate's message or announcement.

▲ Retell or summarize your classmate's message or announcement.

Vocabulary

Position Words

in

out

up

down

Announcements/Messages

Get Ready For Grade 1

Be a good speaker!

Let's Practice It!

Signs

● Listen to the selection.

■ What is the selection about?

▲ Point to each sign. Tell what it means.

★ Why does each stand at the market have a sign? Who will read the signs?

♥ How do the signs help Sandra with her plans?

At a Farmer's Market

Apples
10 for $1

Farmer's market

Corn
6 for $2

Pumpkins
$3 each

Green
Beans
$2 a bag

Carrots
$1 a bunch

111

Objectives
- Point out groups of spoken words that begin with the same sound.
- Say the sound at the beginning of spoken one-syllable words.

Let's Listen for

Initial Sounds

Read Together

● Point to the table. Say, "two tan tables." What sound do you hear at the beginning of those words?

▲ Find three things in the picture that begin with /t/.

★ Name other words that begin with /t/.

READING STREET ONLINE
BIG QUESTION VIDEO
www.ReadingStreet.com

112

Objectives
- Identify and put pictures of objects into categories.

Comprehension

Envision It!

Classify and Categorize

READING STREET ONLINE
ENVISION IT! ANIMATIONS
www.ReadingStreet.com

114

Envision It! | Sounds to Know

Read Together

Mm

motorcycle

Tt

turtle

READING STREET ONLINE
ALPHABET CARDS
www.ReadingStreet.com

Phonics

Initial *m*, Initial *t*

Letter Sounds I Know

M m   M m

T t   T t

High-Frequency Words

Words I Can Read

to

a

Sentences I Can Read

1. I am a little .

2. I 🏃 to 🏫 .

117

Objectives
● Know upper- and lower-case letters. ● Point out the common sounds that letters stand for. ● Know and read at least 25 often-used words.

Phonics

I Can Read!

Decodable Reader

● Consonant Tt
(with rebus)
tiger
turtle
turkey
toad
toucan
tadpole

■ High-Frequency Words
I
to
a

▲ Read the story.

READING STREET ONLINE
DECODABLE eREADERS
www.ReadingStreet.com

Decodable Reader 6

Let's Go

Written by Liz Cristie
Illustrated by Larry Jordon

I walk to a tiger.

I walk to a turtle.

I walk to a turkey.

I walk to a toad.

 I walk to a toucan.

I walk to a tadpole.

 I walk home.

Objectives
- Identify and put pictures of objects into groups. • Retell the important facts from a selection heard or read.
- Connect what you read to your own experiences, to other things you have read or heard, and to the world around you.

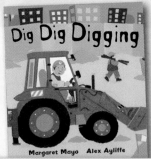

Big Book

Envision It! | Retell

Think, Talk, and Write

1. How are the trucks in *Smash! Crash!* and *Dig Dig Digging* different?

   Text to Text

2. Which things belong together? ↻ Classify and Categorize

3. Look back and write.

Objectives
- Listen closely to speakers by facing them and asking questions to help you better understand the information.

Let's Learn It!

Vocabulary

- Talk about the pictures.

- What do you see that is big? What is little?

- Who is tall and who is short?

Listening and Speaking

- Where do AlphaBuddy's stories take place?

Vocabulary

Words for Sizes

big

little

tall

short

Respond to Literature
Drama

Be a good listener!

Let's Practice It!

Folk Tale

● Listen to the folk tale.

■ What can you tell about the third little pig?

▲ What does the wolf say each time he comes to a house?

★ What lesson do the first two pigs learn?

♥ Why do people like to read or listen to this story?

The Three Little Pigs

Words for Things That Go

airplane

bike

truck

car

bus

van

boat

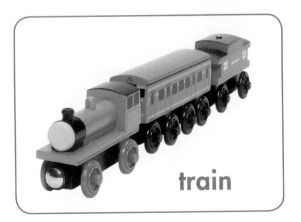

train

Words for Colors

white

purple

brown

green

black

pink

blue

red

yellow

orange

Words for Shapes

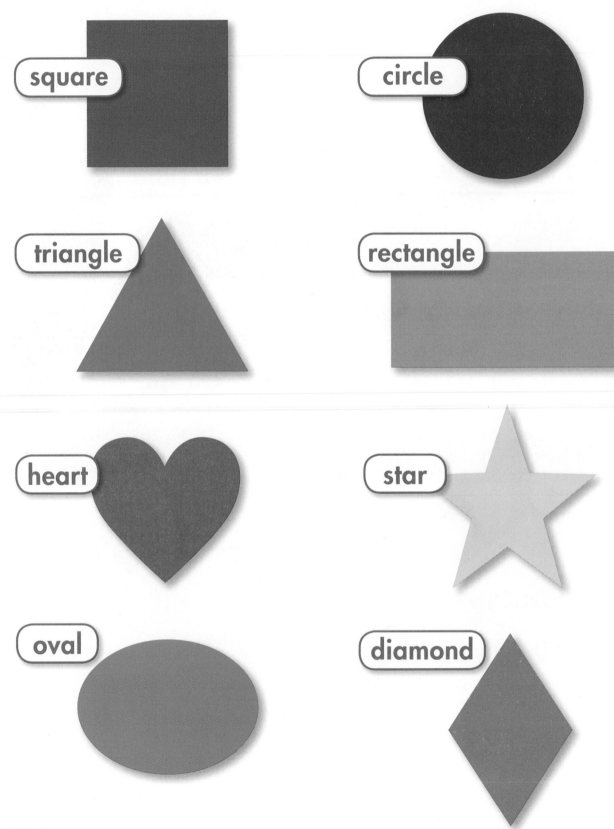

square

circle

triangle

rectangle

heart

star

oval

diamond

134

Words for Places

school

home

park

train station

police station

fire station

post office

library

Words for Animals

lion

mouse

puppy

dog

cat

duck

turtle

kitten

chick

hen

rooster

bird

136

butterfly

fish

whale

caterpillar

bear

panda

beaver

calf

cow

Words for Actions

skip

walk

run

fly

swim

ride

jump

hop

138

Position Words

up

down

in

out

on

around

over

under

My Classroom

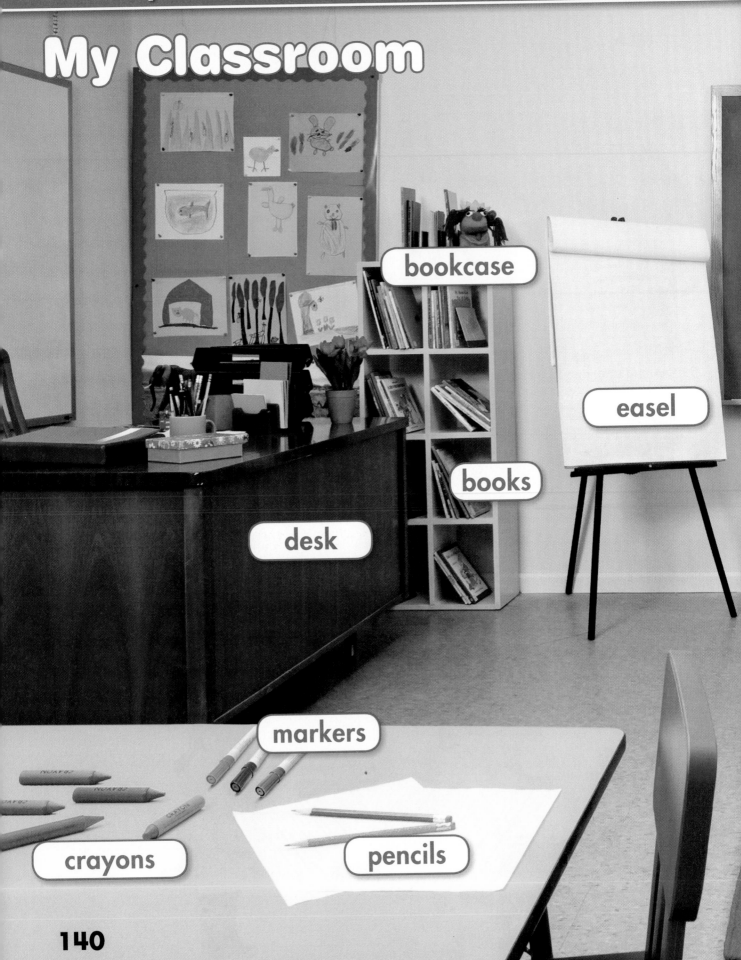

bookcase

easel

books

desk

markers

crayons

pencils

teacher

toys

paper

chair

blocks

table

rug

Words for Feelings

happy

frightened

worried

excited

angry

proud

sad

surprised

My Family

mom
mother

dad
father

sister

grandmother

grandfather

brother

Acknowledgments

Illustrations

Cover: Rob Hefferan
12 Manja Stojic
19–25, 300 Maria Mola
30–31 C. B. Canga
32 Stephen Lewis
39–45, 300 Cale Atkinson
48, 89, 108–110 Mick Reid
52 Ariel Pang
59–65, 300 Natalia Vasquez
70–71 Akemi Gutierrez
72 Amanda Haley
79–85, 300 Robbie Short
92 Ken Wilson Max
112 Jamie Smith
119–125, 300 Dani Jones
130–131 John Ashton Golden
300 Wednesday Kirwan.

Photographs

Every effort has been made to secure permission and provide appropriate credit for photographic material. The publisher deeply regrets any omission and pledges to correct errors called to its attention in subsequent editions.

Unless otherwise acknowledged, all photographs are the property of Pearson Education, Inc.

Photo locators denoted as follows: Top (T), Center (C), Bottom (B), Left (L), Right (R), Background (Bkgd)

10 (B) ©Michael Keller/Corbis

28 ©Drive Images/Alamy Images, ©Lew Robertson/Corbis, ©Motoring Picture Library/Alamy Images, Getty Images

29 ©Alan Schein Photography/Corbis, ©Ron Chapple/Corbis

87 (T, C) Jupiter Images

88 ©Andersen Ross/Blend Images/Corbis, ©Derrick Alderman/Alamy Images, ©Ellen Isaacs/Alamy Images, ©Corbis/Jupiter Images

109 ©Jim Craigmyle/Corbis, ©Peter Christopher/Masterfile Corporation

127 (C) ©DK Images, (T) Getty Images

128 ©Corbis/Jupiter Images, Jupiter Images

129 ©ImageState/Alamy Images, ©Ron Buskirk/Alamy Images, Jupiter Images

133 (B) Getty Images.